Reviews Toast "Of Politics, Ladies and Bagels," by Gene Zahn

"Gene Zahn's poems are a sweet reminder of a time, not so long ago, when the world felt less complicated, our relationships seemed more meaningful, our communication more heartfelt. I pick up his book and read a few of them whenever I need a good dose of that...or just a good chuckle."
Sam Rose, TV Producer and writer, author of "The Way Back - Heal Your Self, Heal The World"

"A wonderful collection of poetry. It made us both laugh and cry. We would recommend it to all our friends and family."
Shelly, sculptress, and Bill Perel, retired CEO

"Gene Zahn delivers an abundant treasure of whimsical observations. Edgy, insightful, entertaining. "
Joe Siegman, Author, "Jews and Sports"

"Zahn's poetry embraces and honors all the pivotal moments of life – from a child's eye, to a soldier's angst, to a young man's dreams and thoughts. His words will jump into your heart, instilling wit, laughter, gratitude and nostalgia for what was and could be. Thank you, Gene. You have inspired me to notice the particulars, enjoy the humor in subtleties, and appreciate the evolution of life."
Lisa Boren, "Happily married mom," Honors: Phi Beta Kappa and Magna Cum Laude

Of Politics, Ladies and Bagels
By Gene Zahn

Edited and designed by Ina Hillebrandt

Published in the United States of America by Pawpress
Brentwood Village ● PO Box 492213
Los Angeles, CA 90049

© 2012 by Gene Zahn
All rights reserved. No portion of this book may be reproduced in any form whatsoever without the written permission of Pawpress, except in the case of brief excerpts published in critical reviews or articles. Inquiries concerning all other uses should be directed to Pawpress at: annap@InasPawprints.com

Library of Congress Control Number: 2001012345

ISBN 978-1-880882-17-7

a PAWPRESS book
InasPawprints.com

Of Politics, Ladies and Bagels

Poetry Provocative and Punny

Gene Zahn

Edited by Ina Hillebrandt

DEDICATION

With my deepest respect and love, I hereby dedicate this book in memory of the most beautiful and most wonderful girl I have ever known, Judith Zahn.

TABLE OF CONTENTS

- DEDICATION IV
- **THOUGHTS POLITICAL** 5
  - WORLD HISTORY 6
  - A MAPMAKER'S LAMENT, 1994 7
  - THE CALL TO ARMS 10
  - AT THE GRAVE OF A SOLDIER 11
  - I WALKED PAST TREES 12
  - THE PATH TO PEACE 13
  - REQUIEM 14
  - BAKED POTATO 15
  - CALIFORNIA POLITICS 16
  - BELLS 17
  - OFF TO THE WARS 18
- **WHEN I WAS A KID, OK, AND A LITTLE OLDER** 21
  - THE BRONX ZOO (THE YEAR 1930) 22
  - IN THE JUNGLE 23
  - THE MOST ADMIRABLE PERSON 24
  - MOTHER'S DAY 25
  - MY FAVORITE TIME OF DAY 26
  - MY FIRST KISS 27
  - TEDDY BEARS IN MY CHILDHOOD 28
  - TEDDI BEAR 29
  - SEX AT SIX 30
  - SHAKESPEARE 31
  - THE SUN AND I 32
- **JUST FOR FUN** 33
  - AN ELEPHANT IN MY HOUSE 34
  - THE DOG DAYS 35
  - THE CARD PLAYER 36
  - CLOSED WINDOWS 37
  - THE DANGEROUS SHARK 38

OUT AT THE RANCH 39
NOTES ON A NIGHT OF INTRIGUE 40
CLOGS 41
THE LOS ANGELES DODGERS 42
DONATION TIME 43
EGGS 44
FISH STORY 45
FLORAL EXPERT 46
GESUNDHEIT 47
FOUR SQUARE 48
HARVEY 49
I AM NOT CRAZY 50
I SAILED AWAY 51
LIVING BY REMOTE CONTROL 52
MY NEW HANGOUT 53
THE OUTLAW 54
OWLS 55
PLACING WAGERS 56
THE SILVER CHALICE 57
SNAKE BITTEN 58
A TABLE OF FRUIT 59
THE TEACHER'S CONTEST 60
THANKSGIVING DAY LAMENT 61
BUZZING FLIES 62
TURTLES 63
TIPPING COWS 64

ON BEING SICK 65
WILLIE, MY SICK ACQUAINTANCE 66
NEW AUTO 67

FOR AND ABOUT THE LADIES 69
A GIRL GROWS UP 70
THE ACTOR MAKES A VOW 71
ANYBODY'S MEAT 72
BARK IN THE TREE 73
BEDROCK 74

THE BICYCLE	75
A BIRTHDAY POEM TO MY SISTER-IN-LAW	76
A VALENTINE STORY	77
CHAGRIN	78
DEADLY WEAPONS	79
THE DIRTY OLD MAN	80
ELOPEMENT	81
ETERNAL ATTACK	82
THE FLOW OF LOVE	84
THE GOLFER	85
GONE ARE THE WINDS	86
LOVE EVERLASTING	87
HARRIET	88
VACATION TIME	89
HER FAVORITE COLOR	90
VALENTINE INCLINE	91
I ALWAYS TAKE PRIDE	92
I WOKE UP WITH LAUGHTER	93
A THOUSAND PENCILS	94
HONESTY AND ETHICS	95
THE WORD IS OUT	96
LESSON OF LOVE	97
LOVE'S EMBERS	98
MANHOOD	99
MARRIAGE PLAN	100
OCEAN WAVES	101
SHE HELD MY HAND	102
THE MATTRESS BECKONS	103
THE MEANING OF *BLUE*	104
THE SOUNDS OF THE HARP	105
THE PRICE GOES UP	106
PUSH BUTTON SOUND	107
PAULINE WAS A HUSSY	108
PICKLES	109
PINEAPPLE	110

ROLLING SURF 111
ROMANTIC BREAKUP 112
THE SAUNA 113
MARRIAGE 115
AUTUMN 116
THROUGH WINTRY WINDS 117
COUPLET FOR A COUPLE 118
RETURN OF LOVE 119
GONE ARE THE WINDS 120
ETYMOLOGICAL FUTILITY 121
SEPTEMBER NINETEENTH 122
NOTES FOR THE WIFE OF A MARRIED TRAVELING SALESMAN 123
MARRIAGE FAUX PAS 124
ODE TO JUDE 125
THOUGHTS WHILE SEPARATED FROM HER 126
WHEN YOUR HUSBAND LEAVES TOWN 127
A VALENTINES DAY POEM 128
YOUR LIPS HAVE BEAUTY UNSURPASSED 130
SPLEND'ROUS IS THE MIGHTY SEA 131
JUDY'S BURIAL 132
GOODBYE, MY LOVE 133
ABOUT GENE ZAHN 135

THOUGHTS POLITICAL

WORLD HISTORY

In recognition of this world's mystery,
It has been noted that bagels can change world history.
If world leaders would eat a bagel a day,
It definitely could keep any army at bay.

Instead of fighting a war so vicious,
Every leader should eat a bagel delicious.
And if they already had eaten and stuffed their soul,
They would have room to eat the bagel hole!

A MAPMAKER'S LAMENT, 1994

Mapmaker, Mapmaker, draw me a map
But you better put on your thinking cap!
If you don't, I think that you'll be hapless
And in '94, we'll be mapless.

Will there be cities left in Serbia
Or will it become all suburbia?
Will peace be absolutely kosher
When the fighting stops in all of Croatia?
What will happen to the Confederation
That was once was so rosy red a nation?
The Confederation of States Independent,
Extremely restive, extremely repentant!
What about Latvia, Lithuania, Estonia?
Is Yeltsin for real, or simply phonier?
Are gone for good, Messrs. Stalin and Lenin?
Do they no longer with red ink, dip their pen in?

Will a most reluctant Albania
Become a part of southern Romania?
Will the memory of an unsteady Bulgaria
Become part of a yet unwritten aria?
And the spectacle of gladiators in the Coliseum
(I'd rather watch 'em than be 'em).
I guess it's a question that now is moot
Whether or not to give Italy the boot!

Will West Germany remain with Germany East?
Will they own the land or have it leased?
Can they ever get rid of their witches' coven
By pushing it into an unused oven?

Mapmaker, Mapmaker: Give me a break!
Will the world become just one big wake?

If ever Paris should not remain,
I would become swimmingly in Seine.
With one big wish and a heaving sighful,
Let eternally stand the Tower Eiffel
Would it not be a thought most callous
If something should happen to Buckingham Palace?

Let the London Bridge never fall
And be replaced by a shopping mall!
And don't forget Ireland, north and south;
Don't give me your lip or your big mouth!
Don't poke at my eyes; don't bite off my nose;
I want to see where the Shannon flows!
Will Turkey be trying to seek a strong peace?
Or will they dirty their hands by dipping in Greece?
Safe for now is Scandinavia;
I guess they have their private savior.

Mapmaker, Mapmaker, what do you say?
Has our world become just one big bidet?

There's the Middle East, land of the Pharaohs,
Civilization's cradle, the straits and narrows.
Will Israel remain with Golan one?
(A tougher feat than a hole-in-one.)
And Arabs that may have pants with ants in
Think the Gaza strip is dirty dancin'.
Will Kadafi still maintain his beloved Libya
Or will he shoot himself in the tibia?
And for Saddam Hussein and resurgent Iraq,
Do we page General Schwarzkopf and bring him on back?
Does our Eagle's bold wings extend to the Kurds
Or is that bad land, well, just for the birds?

Mapmaker, Mapmaker, without thinking cap,
I think that there's just too many a gap.
Mapmaker, Mapmaker, you are capless
And '94 will just have to be mapless!

1994

THE CALL TO ARMS

While others probe the country's problems
And shatter commies, spooks, and goblins,
It seems to be my only mission,
These troubled days of nuclear fission,
To try with utter fascination
To fully love each lass in nation!

AT THE GRAVE OF A SOLDIER

Let tears not fall upon my grave,
For pity can no longer save
My soul or give me lips to talk
Or eyes to see or limbs to walk.
No, if your wails must break the night
Above my bed, your sobs to fight
The very breath of hope that lies
Within the heart of man, your sighs
Should be for those who still must meet
The slashing rains, the knifing sleet,
The winds of war that storm the earth
To place a curse on ev'ry birth.
Condole not me, but those in life
For I no longer share your strife!

I WALKED PAST TREES

I walked past trees and through the brush,
Past playing streams that broke the hush
Of quiet hills and virgin dales,
Marked only by forgotten trails.
Above there was the warming sun,
Caressed by clouds that had begun
To float through space with sails of white
To thrill the soul and blind the sight.

And as I walked alone in peace,
I wondered why man cannot cease
To bring back words like war and strife
To make a mockery of life.
Why can't my fellow man and I,
Believing there's no need to die,
Agree to forge a golden plan
To guarantee man's love for man?

THE PATH TO PEACE

Will we forget that path to peace
In coming days, when men will cease
To bring to mind the hearts that bled
Along the path that still is red
Not with fresh roses breathing spring,
But sticky blood sucked from a thing
That once we knew to be a lad
With eyes alive and heart so glad?

Will we forget that path we tread,
Strewn with the bodies of our dead?
Do we give honor to their souls
By making war and strife our goals?
And will we mock them with the howls
Of booming guns that split the bowels
Of this tired world, and with it all,
The path to peace, beyond recall?

REQUIEM

The setting sun surrenders to
Approaching night with gloaming hue;
The weary worker wends his way
Toward home to greet the end of day.
The peaceful hush of evening's birth
Reflects the quiet of the earth.
Gone is the toil, the trying test;
Home is the man, his soul to rest.

BAKED POTATO

I wish I knew how to bake a potato;
I'd send a slice to ev'ry member of NATO
And finally there would be no mystery
On how to change the world's history.

Wouldn't it be great and very nice
If I could send a well-cooked slice?
Forget all treaties and all lend-lease;
There now would be only world-wide piece!

CALIFORNIA POLITICS

Of all rainbow colors, brown is the greatest;
It's steeped in the past and is the latest!
I further will say to one and to all
Brown is great through spring, winter, summer, and fall!

Of all the colors we see in the rainbow,
The romantic hue of every sane beau,
It has to be brown, a color classic;
It flies in the sky — and none get airsick!

I further will say to one and to all
Just check all the polls—and just this past fall—
The proof is so clear that Brown is the best!
Ev'ry foe did fail; Brown won ev'ry test.

Was Brown a hit man?
Just ask Meg Whitman!

BELLS

We need bells to lull us to sleep;
We need bells to make us respond like sheep.
We need bells to awaken us, too;
We need bells to warn us that a few
Are seeking our dollars with or without cause
And bells to warn us and to obey our laws.

Bells are our friends and are not our foes
And this ding-a-ling brings these lines to a close!

OFF TO THE WARS
(When an Army reservist is called to
active duty for two weeks)

I'm off to the wars, I'm off to the wars,
The cannons and shells, the bellowing roars;
No quarter I ask, no pity I seek;
(I'll see you, my love, just after this week).

These orders to you, concise and so neat,
May cause you to taste both bitter and sweet;
Remember this, Love, they're not made for me—
They're made to protect naive little thee.

The first rule is this—there's no need to balk—
Relentlessly, dear, the foe I will stalk;
I'll capture the men when up at the front;
There's no need for you to enter the hunt!

While bugles' soft tunes will flow to my ear,
It may come to pass a sweet sax you'll hear;
Then go out to dance, if this thrills your heart;
It's all right to dance, but two feet apart!

When heroes are made, I'm first on the line;
The foe I will face from here to the Rhine.
I'll cover the front—at least that's my aim—
Make sure that you do exactly the same!

The next rule is fun, so easy to keep;
You may kiss and kiss (I'll not say a peep);
Your kisses may be—dom de de de dom—
All times, any place, as long as it's your mom!

If neck is your forte, then neck if you wish
(I personally know it's rather delish);
It's okay to neck when there's a blue moon
That shines from eleven A.M. to noon!

When out for a drive and comes time to park
And you're with Tyrone or Cary or Clark,
It's all right to spoon till dawn starts to crack
If you sit in front and he sits in back!

The final rule is: Despite Al and Bill
And Charlie and Dave, Ed, Freddy, and Gil
And Henry and Irv, just please take it easy;
Don't ever forget spectacular GZ!

I'm off to the wars, I'm off to the wars,
The cannons and shells, the bellowing roars;
When things get too tough, I'll turn my two cheeks
And see you, my love, in two little weeks!

WHEN I WAS A KID, OK, AND A LITTLE OLDER

THE BRONX ZOO (THE YEAR 1930)

It was thrilling to hear my Dad say
"We're going to the Bronx Zoo today."
So off we went, my two brothers and I,
To the zoo, which nobody can deny
Was supposed to be the country's best
(By anybody's-- *anybody's*--test).

Into the elephant house to see their hulk,
We viewed the monsters, with all their bulk.
And suddenly, one mammoth lifted his trunk
And into a corner he made a dunk.
He lifted his waste and in one swift maneuver
Maybe he thought he saw President Hoover.
He threw his waste right through the bar
And, lo and behold, *it struck my Pa!*

IN THE JUNGLE

My fondest mem'ry in the jungle
(A happening that I would never bungle);
I met this guy, a friendly cousin?
His name, of course, had me buzzin'.

Related we were — and then he was gone;
My cousin's name? It was *Tar Zahn*!

THE MOST ADMIRABLE PERSON

Through summer, winter, spring, and fall,
The one I respect is at my beck and call.
I admire him for all his great attributes;
I've known him since my earliest roots.

I see him each day when I enter my hall
And look in the mirror on my wall!

MOTHER'S DAY

Her life was devoted to
Her kids and my Dad;
Every breath that she took
Was to make us so glad
To be part of a family
That was together as one.
She was our heaven,
Our stars, and our sun!

MY FAVORITE TIME OF DAY

It was schoolwork time at the hour of six.
I did my homework, then rehearsed some tricks
To make my teacher think: "This guy is great."
And she never would yell if I was late.

I read my homework to the entire class
And tried to impress the prettiest lass.
At the age of twelve was I a social hit?
The light of romance was socially lit!

MY FIRST KISS

My first kiss gave me the feeling
That I shot right through the ceiling!
I heard a hundred cannons roar
And I knew that I wanted more!
My heart was racing like a a galloping horse
And I was engulfed by a great new force!

This new feeling—I could not balk at it!
My first kiss—was delicious chocolate!

TEDDY BEARS IN MY CHILDHOOD

Of all the teddies in my life,
The one I recall caused lots of strife.
Don't take this standing; please have a chair;
I changed my name to Teddy Bare!
And you became my special quarry
'cause I spelled "bear" B-A-R-E.

My problem then began to grow
And you became my biggest foe.
But time heals all, I must admit;
And we got along, like tat for tit!

TEDDI BEAR

I had a crush on Teddi Bear;
I thought that it would never end.
But then I saw my Teddi bare;
It was a *"HE"*— good-bye my friend!

SEX AT SIX

I remember well — at the age of six —
I began a plan to enjoy some tricks.
Our apartment faced a courtyard supreme;
Our neighbors supplied every voyeur's dream.
They never pulled down their available blinds;
I never had seen so many behinds!

But best of all worlds, the best thrills of all,
Were the boobs displayed — at my beck and call.
For my mind so young, it was ecstasy
With no price to pay — just sheer sex to see!
I wanted to taste these fruits so rare —
Forget your apples — I wanted a pair!

SHAKESPEARE

I happily went into the backyard,
Looking for my friend, William Shakespeare.
He promised to be my personal bard
And also to be my personal seer.

It was dark and gloomy, and rather cool,
But I sat down on a wicker chair,
Waiting for the great one at the pool.
He arrived soon after, with his flowing hair.

He listened to my poems, extremely tense,
Then disappeared; *he'd jumped over the fence!*

THE SUN AND I

The very moment I saw the ocean
I quickly applied gobs of lotion.
I truly thought I would be tanned
And threw myself upon the sand.

The tide went out; the tide came in;
Stretched out on the sand was not a sin.
After hours and hours, the sun and I
Became good friends, but bye and bye

I had to leave this piece of coast
Because I became a piece of toast!

JUST FOR FUN

AN ELEPHANT IN MY HOUSE

I awoke from a deepest sleep
And was amazed at what I saw;
An elephant that made me weep—
I was in shock—and dropped my jaw!

He had roamed through all my closets
And threw my clothes onto the floor.
In addition, made deposits—
Quite disgusting, you can be sure!

I thought I would now get even;
I stopped sighin' and stopped grievin';

I grabbed his filth and other junk
And packed it all into his trunk!

THE DOG DAYS

This year don't buy a birthday gift;
Don't even spend a dollar!
The only thing I really need?
I think a new dog collar!

THE CARD PLAYER

When I play cards,
I like to win.
To lose some dough
Is quite a sin.

I went and bought
A mirrored fan;
I'd see all cards
Held by each man.

I thought it went
With great success
Until one day,
I must confess;

They saw my plan
And it was dead.
I'm still in pain
And lie in bed!

CLOSED WINDOWS

I've learned my lesson and my windows are closed;
I can be fully awake or I can easily doze.
I remember the day when this huge orange ball
Crashed through my window and flew into the hall.

There were bits of glass throughout the room
And, of course, thoughts of impending doom.
But I survived the attack; I still was sane
And was I real lucky that I felt no pane?

THE DANGEROUS SHARK

"Don't hate me," said the dangerous shark,
"I only swim; I do not bark.
Don't hate me just because I'm selfish;
Please hate the others, the whales and shell fish!"

OUT AT THE RANCH

I knew there would be trouble, out at the ranch;
Enough to make ev'ry heart flutter and every face blanch.
It wasn't my fault that the heart of a mare
With unmatched feeling, decided to care.

When I placed my saddle upon her back
And lifted my carcass, along with my pack,
When I dug my spurs into her side,
Her head perked up with unusual pride.

Across the valley, with fun we would gallop,
Never missed a step and never would she foul up.
At times we took a leisurely canter;
She was my gal and I was her Santa.

And when we descended upon the stable,
I was her one and only Clark Gable.

I've written many lines, some bad, some fewer;
But never have I written with such horse manure.

NOTES ON A NIGHT OF INTRIGUE

You're Sherlock Holmes,
You're Ellery Queen;
You're Clint Eastwood,
Tough and lean.
I swear you're the best detective in town;
Tonight I shall lay the law down!

CLOGS

Go get some lumber, when you feel real hep,
Then go make some clogs, and step by step,
You will enter a world that only can be
Comfort at last, though somewhat woody.

Your feet will feel great; your legs will vow
To forget leather and laces, and now
Your legs will give thanks from their hearts
and their soles;
Your life will be different with all these new goals.

Though your feet may feel as if they were boiled,
Step by step, you're in a new woild.

THE LOS ANGELES DODGERS

The headlines read "The Dodgers Are Sold!"
Nevertheless, it left me quite cold.
Who cares who owns what on a baseball field?
Who sold what, to someone well heeled?

Let's get the game back to the people;
Let's lower our hearts before the steeple
Of Dodger Stadium; let all root with me.
Let's get back to our routine; let all be rhythmy!

DONATION TIME

They asked for money to save the owls;
I turned them down despite their howls.
They yelled and yelled and tore my suit;
I said to them: "I don't give a hoot!"

EGGS

Have you ever seen a happy egg?
To get an answer, you'd have to beg;
Its end is always a crushing one
And may end up in a boiling bun!

An egg's life is such a painful life;
It is filled with lots and lots of strife;
So be nice to eggs and to their souls;
May they live in piece, in nice warm rolls!

FISH STORY

Have you ever wondered that
Fish are never very fat
Except, of course, the monstrous whales?
The other always carry scales.

FLORAL EXPERT

I can tell you how much I really adore
When the experts agree with one mighty roar
That some flowers are said to be "Oh, so pretty!"
(After all, I grew up in the city.)

I realize my floral knowledge is very shallow;
My floral cognition is extremely fallow.
So if I should clip some stems by error,
Will I eternally face a life of terror?

GESUNDHEIT

Gesundheit is not a word to be sneezed at;
The word, part of our culture, has squeezed at
A rate
Too great
To deny its arrival;
All hail its survival!

Gesundheit is now part of our culture;
To deny it makes one a horrible vulture!

All hail when I begin to sneeze;
Yell *"gesundheit"* and get down on your knees!

FOUR SQUARE

Four square and seven years ago
I decided to make my life aglow.
I would place honesty and truth on my front line;
I would cherish and carry a *"Four Square"* sign.
Forgive me if I close with a very deep sigh;
So what if I'm filled with scotch and some rye!

HARVEY

"Harvey," I said, "What's with the cat?"
"He's my friend," he replied. "Would you like to chat?"
"Heck, no," I said. "Get him out of my home!
"Can't you see, I'm trying to write a poem?"

But Harvey replied: "I thought you're my friend.
"If you want me to leave, then this is the end!"
"That's okay with me. Just call me a louse;
"But I don't want to live in any cathouse!"

I AM NOT CRAZY

I did not believe my half-closed eyes;
I saw a swan, a real surprise.
What was it doing in a subway car?
It attracted eyes from near and far.

And at the very next stop
It left the car in one big hop.
Indeed the swan had left the train.
And I wondered: *was I insane?*

From that time on, I use trolley cars,
Especially when I visit Mars!

I SAILED AWAY

Just as I got to the pier
The boat began to pull away;
Then some guy began to kick my rear
And I began to slip and sway.
I sailed to sea and I have to say
This is the truth; I'm really hip.
The story's done; it ain't no ship!

LIVING BY REMOTE CONTROL

It's great to live by remote control
Especially when saving is not your role.
You can turn on a switch and get just what you wish,
A piece of rare steak or other great dish!
You can turn on a switch to get rid of that boil
Or send a request for a beautiful goil!

It's great to live by remote control
Unless you want to hold onto your soul!

MY NEW HANGOUT

It was with utter passion
That I always followed the latest fashion.
I bought my clothes with lots of moolah
And thought myself as somewhat cooler.

But when this place, a nudist hangout,
Invited me to come and bang out,
I loved my life and new beginning
And when they stared, I left them grinning!

THE OUTLAW

I've taken your car;
I guess I'm a baddie;
But when I play golf,
I do need a caddy!

OWLS

Some people seem to worship owls
And love to hear their annoying howls;
I would like to give them my powerful boot
Maybe because I just don't give a hoot!

PLACING WAGERS

We still have time to place a bet;
The teams are on the field and set
To start the game; so who will win?
Is betting still a mortal sin?
It is no joy to lose a buck;
You can't be sure to have good luck.
A dollar lost? It ain't no fun.
And if you lose, just use a gun;
Don't shoot yourself; don't aim it high.
Just set your sight—the bookie's s thigh!
And if police say you are wrong,
Just knock them down and sing a song.

I'll see you soon, in twenty years,
Back in the stands and leading cheers!

THE SILVER CHALICE

In the land of royal people
I always wanted to approach the steeple
Where the silver chalice was carefully hidden;
To touch it or steal it was truly forbidden.

But a curious mind made me try to steal it
And then proceed to secretly deal it.
I could make a few bucks and then retire
And blame all the crimes on an unlucky buyer!

SNAKE BITTEN

I always have wondered
What it would be like to be a snake;
Would I be spouting real poison
Or would it be fake?
I would scare the pants off people
And they would climb the highest steeple.
I would be proud to have people fear me
When I would hiss for all to hear me.

Only I would know that I'm really a phony;
I'd rather be a much wanted pony!

A TABLE OF FRUIT

I came home from work
And the first thing I saw
Was a table of fruit,
Some cooked and some raw.
My hand grabbed an apple
Along with a grape;
I thought it was shameful
But I couldn't escape.
I then saw a bagel
Lying in wait;
I knew that it faced
Its usual fate.
I grabbed it with all
My heart and my soul;
I ate it with zest,
Including the hole!

THE TEACHER'S CONTEST

When I was asked to teach,
I was asked to select a theme.
I thought it would be of interest:
"To Follow One's Long-Time Dream."

I planned a moneyed contest that all would enter.
One student said he would win the bet!
He was the brightest guy in the center
But lost because his dream was wet!

THANKSGIVING DAY LAMENT

The turkey tried to stay unbowed
A-fightin' and a kickin'.
"Don't kill me!" he cried out aloud.
"Don't kill me, 'cause I'm chicken!"

BUZZING FLIES

If it weren't for billions of flies
The world would be a much smaller size.
There would be much less constant slapping
And much uninterrupted napping.
Strict rules of hygiene? Now unheeded.
But zippers on pants would still be needed!

TURTLES

Walk down a street to find a turtle?
You'll not succeed; they're not too fertile.
They don't satiate their wants or their whims;
They rather sing some religious hymns!

But we can help to raise their desire
Let's sell them books: "How to Light Their Fire!"

TIPPING COWS

My latest gal was a tipping cow
And I imposed my will every then and now.
My latest tip got me into trouble
And I suddenly burst my latest bubble.

I now feel great, hearty and hale;
I'll be tipping again when I get out of jail!

ON BEING SICK

WILLIE, MY SICK ACQUAINTANCE

I said, "Willie, why wear cowboy spurs?"
His answer short, and extremely tense,
"Do you suggest I should wear my furs?"
I said: "Dear pal, you're not making sense."
"I'm mounting my horse, and on the right end."
I said: "There's no horse, only a skateboard."
He replied with a smirk: "I thought you're my friend."
He jumped on the wood and away he soared.

He scooted away, to meet a strange fate;
I guess he entered a white pearly gate!

NEW AUTO

If I had to by a car of my cherce
It would not be black and would not be a hearse!

FOR AND ABOUT THE LADIES

A GIRL GROWS UP

By her own choice, she changed the rules;
She's now the boss of all her fools.
We can't talk back; we can't retort.
We cannot cheat or we'll get caught!
And we will face a vicious fate,
Thrown to the wolves or become shark bait.
And she's a queen and I'm a devil!
How did I sink to this low level?

Release me from this awful state
And I'll ne'er again embrace jail bait!

THE ACTOR MAKES A VOW

I promise to be extremely loyal
All wedding vows I'll sign;
I am not acting, you are my goil!
I'll now remove my *pantomine!*

ANYBODY'S MEAT

I wish that I were a head of cattle.
I'd be a thick piece of good steak that'll
Demand that your mouth just water and drool;
At last you'd be right in calling me "Fuel!"

When placed to your lips, I'd be delicious,
And on your stomach, they wouldn't be suspicious.
I wish I were steak instead of human,
As long as your tummy has some room in!

BARK IN THE TREE

I tied my gal to a lofty tree
And quickly decided to make love;
But I found out much too late
She was just a weakest dove.

In other words, my bark in the tree
Was only valid if I were to pay her fee!

BEDROCK

I asked this gal to take a chance
And she said: "Yes, we should romance."
I thought I'd change my dirty linen
So we could enjoy our promised sinnin'.
But I didn't have time to fix the bed;
It's best the results remain unsaid.

THE BICYCLE

Upon my bicycle, on lover's lane
With great confidence, feeling quite sane,
I suddenly saw in front of me
A beautiful gal in jeopardy!
With great confidence, I hit my brake
And I yelled at her "For goodness sake,
Watch out for that car, just on your right;
I think the driver is somewhat tight!"
She tumbled over; I struck her bike
And she said to me: "You stupid tyke!"
I replied to her: "I saved your hide!"
But my love for her so quickly died.

Some months later, we two got hitched;
We buried our bikes, our lives enriched!
We are so happy, just two plain folks;
We enriched our lives on broken spokes!

A BIRTHDAY POEM TO MY SISTER-IN-LAW

I have a question to ask,
But don't take me to task,
Because it may seem somewhat naughty;
Can it really be true?
Bust, waist, hips, and age, too,
Each equals the figure of forty?

A VALENTINE STORY

My so-called friend made a suggestion
To cure me of constant indigestion.
"We have for you something great:
"A very special Valentine date!"

I quickly accepted with apprehension
But looked forward with lots of tension.
I finally met--ugh--the girl of my dreams?
She was part of professional wrestling teams!

Her face was ugly and rather awful;
In no way was she cute, and perhaps unlawful!
Her lips were messy and her nose was twisted;
If her face touched mine, I could never have kissed it!

So I will have to wait until Valentine next year
And hope to replace my bitten off ear!

CHAGRIN

She loved my looks, she loved my style;
To hold my hand, she'd walk a mile.
She was my gal, I was her man;
To marry me, was her great plan.

But then I met a dizzy blonde;
Within her net, I felt a bond.
And so I called old Number One
And meekly said, "Our time is done."

To my surprise, she quickly said:
"That's fine with me, I thought you dead!"
But worst of all, to my chagrin,
My new found friend just packed me in!

DEADLY WEAPONS

I did not fear; I did not cringe;
She said she'd fire despite our binge.
Loaded up with weapon deadly
She then took aim; fired a medley
Of ammo right at my hip bone;
I called *police*, from my cell phone!

She fired and fired some paper clips,
Carefully aimed below my hips.
I cried out loud with great power
But stood up straight, did not cower.
I did survive but did lay down—
And suddenly we went to town!

THE DIRTY OLD MAN

He was such a dirty old man
And I was not his biggest fan;
And when he made a pass at my gal
And at my wife,
I decided to give him a shortened life.

One day he looked out from his second floor shop
To see if the rain had come to a stop.
I decided to give him a sudden shove
From his office which was just above
A picket fence, protected by wire;
If there should be a witness, I would then shout: "Liar!"

My trial comes up sometime next week;
I must be charming, perhaps rather meek.
If I survive this extremely difficult time,
I will never commit another crime.

If I am sent to a co-ed jail,
I surely won't post any kind of bail!

ELOPEMENT

Why don't we just elope
And, Honey, do be mine?
I'll grab a slice of hope
And drink a glass of whine!

ETERNAL ATTACK

Fight me,
Bite me,

Bomb me,
Harm me,

Claw me.
Paw me,
--------But love me!

Strike me,
Psych me,

Wreck me,
Deck me,

Hurt me,
Dirt me,
--------But love me!

Ignore me,
Gore me,

Bash me,
Clash me,

Hate me,
Berate me,
-----------But love me!

THE FLOW OF LOVE

It was at a waterfall that I fell in love;
The thunderous sound came from the floor above;
My heart began to beat most heavily
In the men's room at Wilshire and Beverly.
Was this a sign from Mr. Cupid?
Or was I really very stupid?
To think my heart would go splitter splatter
As the water flushed; it didn't matter.
Love finds its way in strangest places;
True love will form a solid basis!

THE GOLFER

I'm off to the field, I'm off to the field—
The niggardly earth that refuses to yield.
While you're at home, in royal splendor,
I'll be at work with muscles tender.

I'm off to the field, where it isn't so cool:
With you in my heart, I will win my duel!

GONE ARE THE WINDS

Gone are the winds, the grey-black skies;
The storms are past. No more good-byes
Encased in stony words and tones;
Gone are the tears, the soft-cried moans,
For joy and laughter now become
A part of us, perhaps sent from
The stars, the moon, the sun above
To fill our hearts and lives with love!

LOVE EVERLASTING

I love my golf,
I love my booze;
But my true love
Is really youse!

Some people win,
Some people lose;
I always win
'Cause I love youse!

One animal barks,
Another moos;
I always purr
'Cause I love youse!

It ain't in the headlines,
It ain't in the news;
But you can be sure
That I love youse!

You may have visited
A thousand zoos;
But no animal loves you more
Than I love youse!

(I've paid all my dues—
Now let's blow a fuse!)

HARRIET

I wondered how best to control dear Harriet;
Should I tie her down with a cowboy's lariat?
And then I noticed she loved to look at the ceiling
And I did my best to keep her kneeling!

VACATION TIME

I guess I'm sentimental about trips
And the feeling that a swaying train gives to my legs and hips;
I know, too, I'm more than a little emotional
When I'm about to embark on a voyage oceanal.

Most important, though, I want to clearly admit
(Rarely, but rarely, do I an infinitive split)
That any vacation would be a thousand fold more desirable
And I say this without being under the influence of scotch, bourbon,
or being even the slightest degree ryeable.

If you could share any two or more weeks with me
Playing tennis in the daytime and in the nighttime dancing to some rhythmy
Music under the stars and moon and clouds—no rain—
I could stand it, feeling little or no pain.

Needless to say, I would enjoy this so much
Provided, of course, that we go Dutch.

HER FAVORITE COLOR

It seemed she loved all things turquoise,
'Specially when a gift from boys.
Her fav'rite color? Somewhat odd.
(My fav'rite color? Her pure white bod!)

VALENTINE INCLINE

For you I'd climb the highest peak
Of any Cal incline;
So hear me when these words I speak:
Please be my Valentine.

I'd keep your gauge of gasoline
At level of gallon nine.
I'll keep your car so very clean;
So be my Valentine.

And when it comes to beer that's first,
It's Bud or Ballantine;
But only you can quench my thirst,
So be my Valentine.

If I were asked to pick and choose
Just any gal in line,
I'd pick on you; I could not lose—
Please be my Valentine!

I ALWAYS TAKE PRIDE

I always take pride in the skills I have;
Some are good and some are bad.
But she is great and full of charm;
I know she's like a loaded bomb!

I always feel I'm the best of men
But damn, I keep yelling: *"NOT AGAIN!"*

I WOKE UP WITH LAUGHTER

I couldn't believe I woke up with laughter;
It was only four or five minutes after
We turned away from a solid session.
I did not rescind my last confession:
"I shall be careful not to harm you."
But then I said, "I'm going to bomb you!"
We started to go with utter passion,
With acts of love (some out of fashion).

When it was over, with a keen sense of shame,
We began again and replayed our game!

A THOUSAND PENCILS

She said I was her real Clark Gable
And led me to a big round table;
She pointed out scores of pencils,
Side by side with a hundred stencils.

"The table's full," she shyly said,
"The other room has a great big bed."
She asked of me: "Well, what do you think?
If things go well, do I get a mink?"

My love for her quickly diminished;
Our romance was now truly finished.
I grabbed some pencils and left the place
With one sharp point stuck in my face!

HONESTY AND ETHICS

I've always been a four-square model,
The type all women like to coddle.
I live by rules and ring every belle;
I deter them from a life of hell!

Forget all tricks and screwed-up passions;
I give them money and other rations.
Be honest, above all else, be full of charm;
Let your life be a living psalm.

But don't get caught in a ringing tide;
The last thing you need? *A full-time bride!*

THE WORD IS OUT

Of all the words beginning with "L"
I quickly state one that comes from hell.
"What is that word," I can hear you ask?
(Please wait until I put on my mask.)
That word, I say, and I quote: "*Ladies*"
That word, I add, began in Hades!

LESSON OF LOVE

If you want her to teach you what sex is,
Just go out and buy her a Lexus.

LOVE'S EMBERS

Thrust not my heart into the fire
Or burn my love with careless ire,
For thou would see thy actions rash
And then would seek to kiss my ash!

MANHOOD

If you want to have fun and cause quite a stir
Like the kind that is caused by a him and a her,
Grab a partner and on the floor or a bench
Forget the past and become a *mensch!*

MARRIAGE PLAN

At last, at last, I've found a plan
To help us get closer and closer;
You do the buying at Tiffany's
And I'll buy at the local grocer!

OCEAN WAVES

The ocean liner loved to rock and roll
And so I began to reflect the toll
Of those monstrous waves that made me sick.
And then I lost my beautiful trick.
She went overboard in a second's time;
I lost my true love — what a monstrous crime.
I was now alone, without my great pal.

Later that night, I fell in love
With another great gal!

SHE HELD MY HAND

She held my hand
And after a pause,
She said she loved
The look of my floors.

And then she winked
With lots of feeling,
"It's time I love
The look of your ceiling!"

THE MATTRESS BECKONS

The mattress beckons one and all;
Do not resist; prepare to fall.
Go rest thy weary bones and stretch;
But first of all go out and fetch
A glamour queen to share your bliss,
Perhaps to share a ling'ring kiss.
And who can say what could arise
To glorify both hearts and eyes!

THE MEANING OF *BLUE*

Blue can mean sadness
And sometimes badness.
It can be courage—or even winning;
Or it can be a degree of sinning.
If *blue* can mean almost anything,
Why don't you and I have a fling?
It may even turn out to be great
And you may ask for another date.
And I even will pay for every cost
Or, who knows, you may say "Get lost!"

Then I will always remember you
Though I'll always be feeling *blue!*

THE SOUNDS OF THE HARP

I thought she would listen to the sounds of my harp;
(We had just feasted upon a delicious carp).
I thought she's my gal and I forced her to listen
While my heart was beating like a runaway piston.
I thought the music would see my scheme hatch
And the lock on her heart would make her unlatch;
But I was wrong; her love bells didn't ring
And she finally called me a square ding-a-ling!

THE PRICE GOES UP

This week I'm looking forward
Perhaps to make a lot more money;
I'll rent my body and my soul
If I can find some good-looking honey.

And if she comes up with twenty-five,
I'll even act as if I'm alive.
I hope my fee is not too high—
I'm talking cents *(I'm quite a guy!)*

PUSH BUTTON SOUND

I did not know she had installed
A button sounder in our bed.
I did not know what it was called
Or how it worked; we had just wed.

The sound it made was instant laughter;
It sounded off a minute after!

PAULINE WAS A HUSSY

Pauline was a hussy
With a strong clientele;
She never was too fussy
On her merry way to hell.

Of morals, she had rather few
But she truly loved her food;
She always ate without a clue;
And became just one fat dude!

When Pauline saw her double chin,
She bought a trampoline;
She turned out real, real thin
And became a tramp so lean!

PICKLES

It may be sour, it may be sweet;
But either way, its taste is neat.
Just grab a knife and eat a slice,
Especially when it's placed on ice.

You'll fall in love and I'll be there
And we will have a life to share!

PINEAPPLE

I love pineapple, you can be sure;
When I finish one, I then want more.
It's a slice of life, not to be lost
Regardless of price; forget the cost!

Just follow your wish; eat ev'ry slice.
Whether it's rainy; whether it's nice.
When you are finished, eat one piece more;
If one piece falls down, eat off the floor!

Just one thing's greater than one more hunk;
It's sharing with you — *a narrow bunk!*

ROLLING SURF

The river was wide and rather deep;
I made up my mind, to take a chance,
To impress my gal, I'd take a leap
And give one good shot to our romance.

I began to fear the rolling surf
And so I returned to solid turf.
But she did not care for our romance
Until she noticed I'd lost my pants.

I had come ashore, with plans quite bold
And hoping my gal had not turned cold.
I had come ashore with hopes held high
And wearing only a really wet tie!

So my story ends, my tale is gone;
And do you believe this twisted yarn?

ROMANTIC BREAKUP

How in the world could you leave me cold?
I never met anyone so terribly bold.
In all our years of dirty dancing,
I always was great in our romancing!

The time will come when you'll regret
That no longer will I keep you out of debt!

THE SAUNA

She had followed me all day and, finally, into the sauna.
She was thrilled that she had forced me into a corner.
She said: "You can't wiggle out 'cause I've hidden your pants;
Your only way out is to continue our romance!"

I admitted that I absolutely had no cherce...
And so, this is the end of the verse.

MARRIAGE

AUTUMN

The rich array of rainbow hues
From autumn's palette seems to fuse
All beauty eyes have ever found.
The tawny leaves that fall to ground
Are notes of sympathy sent by
The fresh north wind, whose mellow sigh
Becomes the requiem to mark
The death of summer, cold and stark.

THROUGH WINTRY WINDS

Through wintry winds and chilling blasts,
From icy fields of frost, we've passed.
From heat-filled valleys, scorched and seared,
We've come. And still we're lost; we've feared
Not knowing which path to take.
We've split our souls; our hearts do ache
With doubt, for what is wrong or right?
Like Sinai's children, through the blight
We've come, the promised land so near;
And yet we turn our backs and veer
Away from warmth and shining sun,
Becoming two instead of one.

COUPLET FOR A COUPLE

You are my love, my one and only;
Without you I am very lonely!

RETURN OF LOVE

A sea of blue, a cloudless sky,
The splend'rous sun to strike the eye;
Within my heart there was the calm
Of peaceful skies — and no alarm.
But though horizons seemed so clear
And though within I felt no fear,
The storm clouds formed and seas of blue
Became a sickly grey-black hue.
The shrieking wind, the lightning's flash,
The drenching rain, the thund'ring crash
All joined in one; within this strife
I thought I reached the end of life.

But winds will die and clouds will leave.
The rains must stop—and on that eve
I hope to God to share my name,
And to the world I will proclaim:
"At last my life will now begin!"
And not the words, "What might have been."

GONE ARE THE WINDS

Gone are the winds, the grey-black skies;
The storms are past. No more good-byes
Encased in stony words and tones;
Gone are the tears, the soft-cried moans,
For joy and laughter now become
A part of us, perhaps sent from
The stars, the moon, the sun above
To fill our hearts and lives with love!

ETYMOLOGICAL FUTILITY

What words reflect the golden spark
Of stars? Or when can thoughts of dark
On white be deeper than the blend
Of blue-green seas? Do some words tend
To bring to mind the mellow glow
That fuses day with night, the flow
Of streams that carelessly divide
The wooded green, the rushing tide
That throws is fury waves upon
Resisting rocks?   What thoughts placed on
The smoothened flat of nothingness
Compare with autumns soft caress
Of wine and toast, of green and gold?
These beauties only eyes behold
And not the muted hand on quill.
And so with thee, what words can fill
My heart and mind, to picture thee
As thou art here, to capture me?

SEPTEMBER NINETEENTH

The days may pass; the years may run.
Time matters not, for we are one.
Our love's forever, timeless, true,
Reborn each moment, exciting, new.
You are my life, you are my life!
I love thee so, my wife, my wife!

NOTES FOR THE WIFE OF A MARRIED TRAVELING SALESMAN

From now on, your name is Hungry Herbert;
You have an appetite and you won't curb it.
From every roof and housetop I will blurb it;
You ate my pie and raspberry sherbet!

While I spend my time in Phoenix,
Do you miss my scraps of Kleenex?

Please note that when I leave for San Diego,
My heart stays behind and will in no way go!

When I am flying at thirty thousand feet with Western,
I will be thinking that of all the girls in the whole wide world,
You're the best 'un.

MARRIAGE FAUX PAS

I hate to see you get upset
About a piece of chintz;
And when you get a mirror chipped,
I hate to see you wince.

Now, if you want to be upset,
Just think of your guy, Gene;
For he's the rat that made you change
Your name to Zahn from Green!

ODE TO JUDE

When it comes to your going on a diet,
I don't think you should try it.
Oh, I know that automobiles need overhauling, valve jobs, and
Occasional lubes,
But not your boobs!

Yes, I realize that some vessels are tremendous, like
Aircraft carriers and cruisers, but destroyers are tiny ships,
Like your hips!

And furthermore, your legs are really sleek, like a
Slim cowboy tossing a lasso;
Truly, a Picasso!

So everyone —from the most southerly part of Chile
All the way to Cape Cod —
All hail, all hail, your magnificent bod!

THOUGHTS WHILE SEPARATED FROM HER

The clouds go swiftly by, and through
The sky I race to offer you
My hand and heart, to share the night.
The moments pass and soon the flight
Will find your arms, your lips, your smiles;
These promises reduce the miles
That sep'rate us, (though we are one);
For love like ours, when once begun,
Has spanned the earth and space and time
And placed our thoughts and hearts in rhyme!

WHEN YOUR HUSBAND LEAVES TOWN

When your husband leaves town,
His heart doesn't go with him;
He leaves it with you
To maintain its proper rhythm!

A VALENTINES DAY POEM

Your lips are like rubies;
They're red as a rose.
Your legs were made
To advertise hose.
Your nose is as straight
As a cleric's mind;
With all due rev'rence,
All hail thy behind!
The rest of your figure,
You win—all hands down.
To sip of your beauty
Without or with gown,
Beats Venus de Milo's;
Is like drinking rare wine;
So today I exclaim:
Be my Valentine!

If anyone's perfect,
God-like, it's you;
Like baseball and pie,
Like red, white, and blue
Your mind's a computer,
A program complex;
You're a million in cash,
A billion in checks.
Your only big problem,
Not run of the mill,

Is that your dear husband
Ain't in Ross Perot's will.
Though champagne is your drink
And mine's Ballantine,
Today I exclaim:
Be my Valentine!

YOUR LIPS HAVE BEAUTY UNSURPASSED

Your lips have beauty unsurpassed
As though they've kissed the setting sun;
The tender rays of warmth they cast
Must bleed the hearts of those they've won.

I want so much the thrills I need,
The pressing lips, the restless tongue,
The crushing force that know no heed,
The sweetest song man's ever sung.

If these to me have been denied,
I cannot live; my soul had died!

SPLEND'ROUS IS THE MIGHTY SEA

Splend'rous is the mighty sea!
The world has never felt a force
So great, a power flowing free
Beyond control with no set course;
It has its tides escape the shore
And then proclaims its mastery
When it returns with rolling roar.
At times it finds tranquility
Then suddenly it can become
A whirling, crashing sea of storm
And just as quickly rushes from
This truc'lent mood and changes form
Into a lake serene and clear;
While currents pull and hold and yield,
Blend secrets sweet and some austere,
Its mystic deep has much concealed!

Our love is like the mighty sea,
Rushing, calming, storming, still;
Love's waves and winds may not agree,
May swirl and shriek and yet they will
So soon surrender to a sea
Of love, profound and pow'f'lly great,
To share our hearts eternally
Our arms, our love, our lives to sate.

Though seas be calm or turbulent,
Our love will be omnipotent!

JUDY'S BURIAL

On this mid-August day in the year 2007,
Judy was buried in our family plot, in New York.
The weather that day was partly cloudy,
With the sun finally winning the weather war.

There were only about fifteen of us attending the short service.
When I began placing earth upon the grave,
The sun hid behind dense, dark clouds.
And the most torrential rain and electrical storm
I had ever experienced suddenly captured the moment.

The lightning was not the usual kind;
The usual zig-zag pattern of lightning was missing;
In its stead was lightning that appeared
As one sheet from horizon to horizon!

When five minutes had elapsed,
And I had covered the grave site with earth,
The rain and lightning stopped
And the sun shone magnificently from horizon to horizon.

Judy had said good-bye.

GOODBYE, MY LOVE

Goodbye, my love, our last long kiss
Is doomed to die in deep abyss
Of mem'ry, ne'er to live again,
Except in mind or heart and when
The fall returns to make too clear
The loving thoughts of yesteryear.

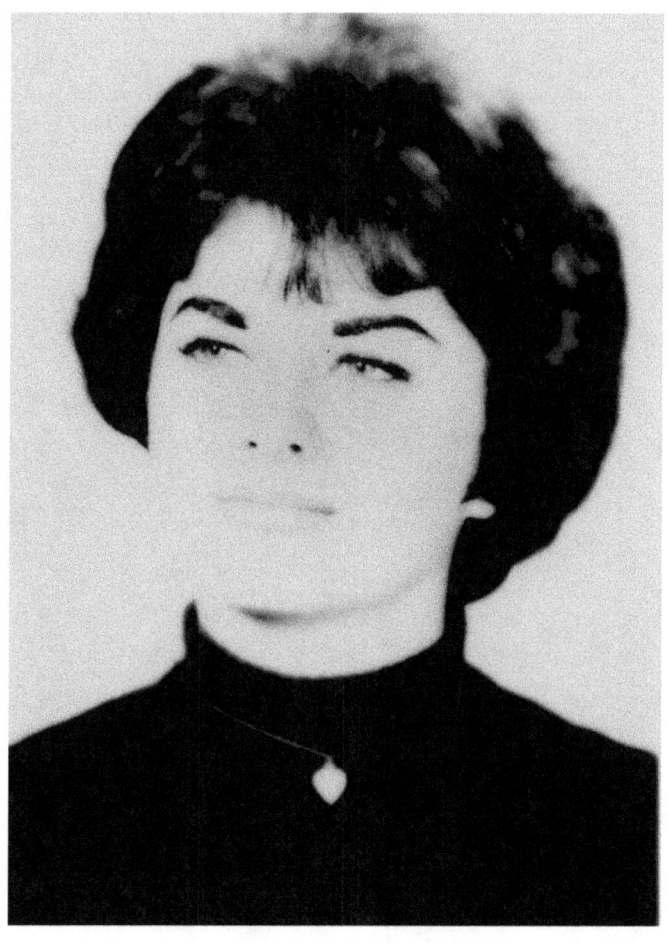

ABOUT GENE ZAHN

The author…who might not be with us today
if it weren't for boots

Gene was born in the Bronx, and grew up "living in the nicest apartment on the block." With borrowed money, his dad had founded International Dress Company, and under his direction it had become the leading dress manufacturer in the United States. But while the family may have lived in the lap of luxury, Gene's parents instilled liberal ideals in their three sons. They always went to public rather than private schools, Gene says, a choice he and his brothers were asked to make each time they were ready to move up to the next level of education, from elementary school on. Their parents were always very proud.

And the sons were proud of their mother and father as well, who were known and respected by everyone they knew as pillars of the community. Their mom made the family the center of her life, and paid a great deal of attention to the children, her husband and their home. About his father, Gene says, "Arriving in the U.S. as a young teenager, my dad worked hard while attending school, and financed his two youngest siblings through college. And he was completely devoted to his sons. Baseball, football, he promoted all the sports with us. We went to these games constantly. We played sandlot also. One year my dad announced a contest, based on grades we were getting on our final report card. I came in with a 92. My middle brother, Paul, had a 94, my oldest brother, Jason, got 102 (really!). My dad said to each of us in turn, 'OK, you win a prize – a box seat at Yankee

Stadium!' Then he gave himself the same prize and we all went to the game. "

Gene's love of words and writing were part of his life from early days in school, where he said he "always did well in compositions." But writing more seriously really began after he graduated from high school. "I started writing in college — NYU University College of Arts and Science campus in the Bronx, where the Hall of Fame is located. In my junior year I became Managing Editor of our college magazine, 'Medley.' I graduated in 1940, at the age of 20. We all knew war was coming on. There was a compulsory ROTC branch at the college, a 2 year commitment, for freshmen and sophomores. If we wanted we could take advanced courses after this in ROTC, and upon completion become 2nd Lieutenants in the Army Reserves. I wanted to do it because I loved the boots – uniforms were great, especially for dating. But at the end of my sophomore year, the Army eliminated the boots, except for members of the Cavalry. This would reduce my appeal with the ladies, so I did not take the advanced course. All those guys who did take it became 2nd lieutenants in the Infantry, the toughest assignment in the Army. A lot of them didn't come back.

"When I was still a sophomore, my dad died. This was 1937. His partner was his next youngest brother, to whom my dad had simply given half the business, some years earlier. When he died, this uncle arranged for the company's valuation to be lowered considerably from its true worth, and then forced my mother into selling her share to him. She received much less than was her due, and we had to move to a lesser place. It was still a nice apartment on Riverside Drive, and my mother had enough to get along, but not in the style of living in which we'd grown up.

"In any case, after I graduated from college, I went to work for my uncle, starting out at minimum wage -- $25 week. He was a very cold person. We (my brothers and I) were not well treated. And we could see the business sliding down. Then Pearl Harbor came along, in 1942. I would be drafted if I didn't do anything, and had been declared 1A. I felt if I enlisted my qualifications would be clearer -- the college degree would help -- and I could work at a better job than if I were a draftee along with a huge number of other recruits. So a month after Pearl Harbor, I went into the nearest recruiting office and asked the officer in charge, 'If I enlist today, where do you send me tomorrow?' He asked, 'Can you type?' I'd taken typing during that last term in high school, so I could touch type. He said, 'You have to get a release from your Draft Board first, then you can enlist. But you have to enlist before we can give you a typing test.' I ran to the Draft Board. They said, 'Zahn, we have you down as already serving in the Navy. We realize our error. Do you still want your release, so you can enlist today?' I said I did. They said 'OK,' gave me the release, and I ran back to the Army recruiting office with the paper in hand. 'So you want to know where you're going tomorrow? If you pass the typing test, you'll be sent to the Brooklyn Cargo Port,' which was a 35 minute subway ride from my house. I enlisted, passed the typing test, and they told me where to go at the Port. I often think about the fact that, for a bit of time, I was the only person in America to be enlisted in two branches of the Armed Services at one time.

"When I got to my post, it was drizzling. 'Private Zahn reporting as ordered, sir,' I said with a salute, on getting to the room where the Captain I was told to report to was to be found.

"'Zahn, what's your nationality?'

"'American, sir.'

"'No, no, I mean….your… nationality.'

"'American, sir…Oh, you mean my religion?'

"'Oh, no, not at all,' the Captain said, and changed the subject.

"In the Army I attended Officers Candidate School for three months, at Mississippi State College. They had a very tough demerit system -- 6 got you dismissed. There was tremendous pressure – the average OCS student got 4, which is what I got. So I didn't get kicked out. While I was there, I wrote for the Starkville newspaper, five miles away from campus. It was a weekly column, talking about life at the school. What I wrote was very serious, to make the school look good. After about a month, I left that work to prepare a graduation booklet for the class, which was a new thing. I think this helped me get sent to the Pentagon. I graduated as a 2nd lieutenant in the Army Transportation Corps, which had just been established. After I served several months in Washington, the Army decided to open a cargo port of embarkation in Philadelphia. So I was sent there from the Pentagon, and served the rest of the war in Philly."

Today Gene is proud to say he attained the rank of captain during the war, stayed in the Reserves for thirty-five more years, and retired as a lieutenant colonel, two steps away from general.

A bit about the love of Gene's life

When Gene was growing up, going through college and then the Army years, clearly there were ladies in his life. But the most significant, and the one who captured his heart forever, was a young woman he met fifteen years after the war ended, Judy Green. You'll find a photo and some beautiful poems dedicated to her in the final section of this book. And here's a snippet about how they came to be a couple. In this story, Gene has returned to the ladies clothing business, and owns his own sales corporation. He is now living in Los Angeles, under contract as regional sales manager for a well known company headquartered on the east coast, Jones New York.

"One day Judy, who was a friend of my chief assistant, appeared in my office. She'd come to visit her folks in L.A. from her home in San Francisco, where my assistant and she had met originally. That day, and while she was in town, Judy came to my office daily to chat with her friend. I found myself engaged in conversation with this attractive young woman occasionally, and on one of these visits, she volunteered some rather interesting information – she resided with a Chinese family that owned the Number 1 nightclub in Chinatown, and they all lived on a Chinese junk in San Francisco Bay. Now I was really intrigued. The third day she was in L.A. she told me it was her last day in town, and that she was leaving for the Bay Area the next day. 'If you're leaving tomorrow, why don't we have a date tonight?' I asked her. 'It might be fun.' She said she didn't think it would be, and left.

"Two years later, I was on a business trip in San Francisco, visiting a small store for potential sales. Judy happened to be an assistant manager in this establishment. She saw me and came out from the back yelling, 'Hey, Gene! Fate sent you here today. This weekend the biggest party of the year is being held in San Francisco. You could do me a tremendous favor! I don't have a date.' I was thrilled. She was beautiful. I was so excited. 'Of course I'll do you this favor.'

"'When you get back to the hotel, would you tell our mutual friend (a guy who was also a friend of my assistant) to call me, because I want him to take me to the party.'

"I was shattered. But she came by my temporary office in San Francisco before I had to leave, and then we started dating. And calling each other every night…"

It's to Judy those of us who love Gene's stories and poems should say thanks. Her death, as painful as it was, and continues to be for Gene, led to his return to writing, which is a way he finds helps him deal with her loss. The poems he pens these days are a mix of the thoughtful and frothful, as he might put it, and I, along with his fans, say "Yippee!"

Ina Hillebrandt,
Editor

If you enjoyed this book, you might also enjoy the following selections from Pawpress…

Sensual Spirit…poetry and thoughts from the place where body and soul meet, by Chrystine Julian. "What a rapturous book! Chrystine Julian weds wit and wisdom, body and spirit, in these poems. Her warmth and humor and deep insight radiate off every page." *Gayle Brandeis, author of "Fruitflesh, Seeds of Inspiration for Women that Write," "Self Storage" and the Bellwether Prize winner, "The Book of Dead Birds."*

Meandering Mindfulness…Poetry from the place where wander and wonder merge. Once again Chrystine Julian paints a colorful world of the sensual, spiritual, political and this time, the "silly," in a book that appeals both to seasoned poets and those who usually read prose. ISBN 978-1-0880882-13-9

Pawprints by Ina Hillebrandt, Amazon.com top seller featured on ABC Nightly News, PBS, etc. From "Moonlit Fox" to "Nose Fur," more than 100 short, short "tails" of close encounters of the furry kind. Uplifts, inspires readers to write, and promotes kindness to animals. Purr-fect gift for animal lovers and pets of all ages. "The stories make you feel you are right there…I love them!" Teresa Proscewitz, Chief Forester, City of LA Dept. of Recreation and Parks. ISBN 1-880882-01-9.

How to Write Your Memoirs — Fun Prompts to Make Writing … and Reading …Your Life Stories a Pleasure! by Ina Hillebrandt. Easy steps and prompts to make organizing those scraps of paper — physical and mental — fun and rewarding, for the writer, family and friends, and possibly, the public! ISBN 1-880882-04-3. "The questions make it easy!" *Gertrude Brucker, Member, Felicia Mahood Senior Center, Los Angeles*

Stories From The Heart, Volumes 1-3 ... Selected stories to delight and inspire readers to create their own memoirs and fiction. Vol. 3 Includes writing tools and carefully selected memoirs — and fiction! — to entertain, and help readers craft their own enchanting life histories. *"Multi-hued, textured tales – from such stuff was woven the American Dream." Marvin J. Wolf, Author of Fallen Angels and many other nonfiction books.* All three **Stories** books compiled and edited by Ina Hillebrandt. Vol. 1 ISBN. 1-880882-07-8. Vol. 2 ISBN 1-880882-08-6 Vol. 3 ISBN 1-80882-04-3.

Go East, Young Man, Go East! *Memoirs of an eyewitness to the oil boom and culture clashes of the Middle East.* By Charles Alan Tichenor, Edited by Ina Hillebrandt. A book of memoirs penned by a witty and informed hand, with tales of political intrigue, spies, cultural exchanges and the effects of black gold on royalty and desert-dwelling Bedouins. ISBN 1-880882-09-4.

Wine, Women, Whispers, by Alan Mintz. Tales by a master storyteller who was kidnapped – twice, almost killed by the best hospital in London…A boxer…Serial entrepreneur… Lover of ladies, food and wine. ISBN 978-1-880882-14-6.

To order any of the books above, please visit Amazon.com, BN.com, other fine online booksellers, or your local bookstore. For more information, and for bulk orders, please visit our website,
http://www.InasPawprints.com

www.ingramcontent.com/pod-product-compliance
Lightning Source LLC
LaVergne TN
LVHW051839080426
835512LV00018B/2957